content

British & North American Readers:
Please note that Australian cup and
spoon measurements are metric. A quick
conversion guide appears on page 63.
A glossary explaining unfamiliar terms
and ingredients begins on page 60.

2 a **fishy** story

When a fish is really fresh it has clear bulging eyes and very black pupils, firm, lustrous skin with tight scales, bright red gills and a pleasant sea smell.

Preparing fish

When you buy fish, all the preparation can be done for you by the fishmonger: the scaling, cleaning and filleting. But what if you've caught the fish yourself, or been given it by a friend? It's always useful to know how to prepare a whole fresh fish.

Scaling fish

Wet the fish (it is easier to scale a fish when it's wet). Lay the fish on a board on several sheets of newspaper (this is to catch the flying scales). Put salt on your forefinger and thumb and hold the fish securely by its tail. Use a fish scaler or a flat-bladed blunt knife and work from the tail towards the head, against the direction of the scales. Turn the fish over and scale the other side, then rinse the fish well and dry with paper towels.

Cleaning fish

Also known as gutting, this is a simple matter of cutting the fish open with a sharp knife along the belly from near the tail to under the head. Pull out all the entrails, wash the cavity of the fish and dry well.

Filleting fish

You can buy special filleting knives, but any long sharp knife with a flexible blade will do. Lay the fish on a board and cut under the front fin across the fish, down to the bone. Insert the knife under the fillet at the head end, and cut flat against the spine, lifting the fillet with your other hand as you go. Move the knife along the spine towards the tail with a 'press and gentle push' motion. Repeat on the other side.

Skinning fish

To skin a fillet, cut a little of the flesh from the skin at the tail end. Hold the skin with salted fingers at the tail end and cut away the flesh, with the knife flat against the skin, not the flesh.

Boning fish

To bone a whole fish, remove the head and cut through the flesh from gills to tail along the belly. Cut through the flesh on either side of the backbone, so the fish can be spread out flat. Avoid cutting into the skin. Spread the fish out flat and cut out the backbone using scissors or a small sharp knife. Trim off rib bones on each side.

Freezing fish

Whole fish: remove gills and gut the fish. Wrap carefully in foil, and avoid piercing foil. Place in freezer bag, remove air, seal, date and label. White fish can be frozen for up to six months, and oily fish for up to three months.

Fillets: rinse under cold water, dry with paper towels. Wrap individually in freezer wrap, stack in appropriate serving portions. Place portions in freezer bag, remove air, seal, date and label. White fish fillets can be frozen for up to six months, oily fillets for three months.

Smoked fish (whole and fillets): these can be frozen in the same way as fresh fish, and will keep for up to three months, but bear in mind that the saltiness will increase during freezing and the smoked flavour will decrease slightly.

4 lemon fish
parcels

4 white fish cutlets
(1kg)

2 teaspoons finely
grated lemon rind

1 tablespoon lemon
juice

2 cloves garlic,
crushed

2 teaspoons grated
fresh ginger

1 small carrot (70g),
sliced thinly

1 celery stick (75g),
sliced thinly

1 small leek (200g),
sliced thinly

3 green onions,
chopped

1 medium lemon
(140g), sliced

Place fish in large shallow dish; brush with
combined rind, juice, garlic and ginger. Cover;
refrigerate 2 hours.

Divide combined vegetables among 4 large
pieces of foil, top with fish and lemon slices.
Seal foil to enclose fish; transfer to baking dish.

Bake in moderate oven about 20 minutes or
until fish is just cooked through.

Per serving fat 5.9g; kJ 1019

salmon

with capers and vinegar

2 tablespoons water

1 small brown onion
(80g), chopped finely

1 celery stick (75g),
chopped finely

4 salmon cutlets
(800g)

1/2 cup (75g) plain
flour

1 teaspoon fennel
seeds

cooking oil spray

1 tablespoon drained
capers

1 tablespoon balsamic
vinegar

Cook water, onion and celery, in large non-stick pan, stirring, until onion is
soft. Remove onion mixture from pan.
Toss salmon in combined flour and seeds; shake off excess flour mixture.
Coat large non-stick pan with cooking oil spray, heat pan; cook salmon,
until lightly browned both sides and cooked as desired. Return onion
mixture to pan with capers and vinegar; cook, uncovered, 2 minutes.

Per serving fat 6.6g; kJ 1219

10 madras curried
fish parcels

2 teaspoons Madras curry paste
1 medium leek (350g), sliced
1 medium red onion (170g), sliced
310g can Corn, Lima Beans and Capsicum, drained
125g snow peas, halved
4 boneless white fish fillets (800g)

Cook paste, leek and onion in large non-stick pan, stirring, until onion is soft. Stir in corn mixture and snow peas. Divide half the vegetable mixture among 4 x 30cm square pieces of baking paper. Top with fish, then remaining vegetable mixture. Pleat baking paper firmly to enclose fish, fold in ends to secure parcels; transfer to baking dish. Bake in moderately hot oven about 20 minutes or until fish is just cooked through.

Per serving fat 7g; kJ 1307

12 spiced fish balls

in tomato sauce

Blend or process fish until minced. Add breadcrumbs, garlic, turmeric, paprika, cumin, coriander, ginger and egg; process until combined. Roll rounded teaspoons of mixture into balls, place on tray. Cover; refrigerate 2 hours.

Add fish balls to simmering Tomato Sauce; simmer, covered, stirring gently, until fish balls are cooked through.

Tomato Sauce Heat oil in large non-stick pan; cook onion and garlic, stirring, until onion is soft. Stir in undrained crushed tomatoes, puree, herbs and water; simmer, uncovered, about 5 minutes or until thickened slightly.

450g white fish fillets, chopped

³/4 cup (50g) stale breadcrumbs

3 cloves garlic, crushed

¹/2 teaspoon ground turmeric

1 tablespoon sweet paprika

1 teaspoon ground cumin

1 tablespoon chopped fresh coriander leaves

1 teaspoon grated fresh ginger

1 egg

tomato sauce

1 teaspoon olive oil

1 medium brown onion (150g), sliced

1 clove garlic, crushed

400g can tomatoes

2 tablespoons tomato puree

2 tablespoons chopped fresh parsley

1 tablespoon chopped fresh coriander leaves

¹/2 cup (125ml) water

Per serving fat 6.8g; kJ 950

spiced fish

with leek, potato and spinach

800g blue-eyed cod fillet

1 teaspoon sweet paprika

3 teaspoons ground cumin

3 teaspoons ground coriander

1/4 teaspoon cayenne pepper

2 large potatoes (600g), chopped

2 tablespoons water

2 cloves garlic, crushed

2 medium leeks (700g), sliced thinly

1 cup (250ml) chicken stock

1/2 bunch spinach (250g), shredded

cooking oil spray

Cut fish into 4 pieces. Combine spices in bowl, coat fish with spice mixture. Cover; refrigerate 3 hours or overnight.

Boil, steam or microwave potatoes until almost tender, drain. Cook water, garlic and leek in large non-stick pan, stirring, until leek is soft. Add potato and stock; simmer, uncovered, 5 minutes. Add spinach, stir until wilted.

Coat large non-stick pan with cooking oil spray, heat pan; cook fish, until browned both sides and just cooked through. Serve fish with vegetable mixture.

Per serving: fat 7.7g; kJ 1535

14 mexican-style fish parcels

4 white fish fillets (800g)

cooking oil spray

2 tablespoons low-fat mayonnaise

1 clove garlic, crushed

3 medium tomatoes (570g), sliced

1 small red onion (100g), sliced thinly

1 tablespoon chopped fresh coriander leaves

1 bottled jalapeno pepper, drained, seeded, sliced

Divide fish among 4 large pieces of foil which have been coated with cooking oil spray, spread fish with combined mayonnaise and garlic. **Top** with tomato, onion, coriander and pepper slices. Seal foil to enclose fish; transfer to baking dish. Bake in moderately hot oven about 20 minutes or until fish is just cooked through.

Per serving fat 6.8g; kJ 1148

snapper cutlets with tomato
herb crust

1 teaspoon olive oil

1 clove garlic, crushed

2 medium brown onions (300g), sliced

2 celery sticks (150g), chopped

3 medium tomatoes (570g), peeled, chopped

3/4 cup chopped fresh parsley

4 snapper cutlets (1kg)

1 teaspoon dried oregano leaves

1 medium lemon (140g), sliced thinly

1/2 cup (125ml) dry white wine

1/4 cup (60m) lemon juice

1/4 cup (15g) stale breadcrumbs

Heat oil in large non-stick pan; cook garlic, onion and celery, stirring, until onion is soft. Add tomato; cook, stirring, until tomato is soft, add parsley; mix well.
Place fish, in single layer, in large non-stick baking dish; sprinkle with oregano. Top with tomato mixture. Place lemon in overlapping slices over tomato mixture, pour over combined wine and juice, sprinkle with breadcrumbs.
Bake, uncovered, in moderate oven about 30 minutes or until fish is just cooked through.

Per serving fat 4.8g; kJ 1198

16 fish burgers
with mustard mayonnaise

4 small firm white fish fillets (600g)

¹/₄ cup (35g) plain flour

1 egg, beaten lightly

1 cup (70g) stale breadcrumbs

cooking oil spray

40cm loaf Turkish bread

100g baby rocket leaves

1 small red onion (100g), sliced thinly

mustard mayonnaise

¹/₂ cup (125ml) low-fat mayonnaise

2 teaspoons lemon juice

1 tablespoon seeded mustard

1 tablespoon chopped fresh chives

Toss fish in flour; shake off excess. Dip fish in egg, then coat in breadcrumbs. Cover; refrigerate 30 minutes.
Coat large non-stick pan with cooking oil spray, heat pan; cook fish, until browned both sides and just cooked through.
Cut bread into 4 pieces, split in half. Toast until browned lightly on both sides. Top half the toasted bread with Mustard Mayonnaise, rocket, fish and onion. Top with remaining toasted bread.
Mustard Mayonnaise Combine all ingredients in bowl.

Per serving fat 14g; kJ 2593

18 fish kebabs with chilli sauce

600g firm white fish fillets, chopped

2 tablespoons soy sauce

2 cloves garlic, crushed

$1/2$ teaspoon grated fresh ginger

2 medium red capsicums (400g), chopped

2 medium green capsicums (400g), chopped

chilli sauce

1 small fresh red chilli, chopped

2 cloves garlic, crushed

1 tablespoon chopped fresh coriander leaves

1 tablespoon fish sauce

1 tablespoon lime juice

$1^1/2$ tablespoons brown sugar

2 teaspoons cornflour

1 tablespoon mirin

$3/4$ cup (180ml) water

Combine fish with sauce, garlic and ginger in bowl. Cover; refrigerate 1 hour. Thread fish and capsicums alternately onto 8 skewers. Cook kebabs under heated grill (or griddle-fry or barbecue) until browned all over and fish is cooked through. Serve with Chilli Sauce.

Chilli Sauce Grind chilli, garlic and coriander to a smooth paste, using mortar and pestle. Add fish sauce, juice and sugar.

Cook chilli mixture in heated dry pan, stirring, until fragrant. Stir in blended cornflour, mirin and water. Stir over heat until sauce boils and thickens slightly.

Per serving fat 4.6g; kJ 1003

baked whiting

with lemon, parsley and garlic

4 medium sand whiting (1.3kg)

2 teaspoons olive oil

2 tablespoons lemon juice

2 tablespoons finely shredded flat-leaf parsley

1 clove garlic, crushed

2 teaspoons grated lemon rind

Place oil in baking dish, add fish. Pour juice over fish, bake, uncovered, in moderate oven about 15 minutes or until cooked through. **Combine** parsley, garlic and rind in small bowl. Serve fish sprinkled with parsley mixture.

Per serving fat 3.6g; kJ 694

24 fish in wine garlic
marinade

4 x 250g whole leatherjacket fish

2 cloves garlic, crushed

1 teaspoon finely grated lemon rind

$1/3$ cup (80ml) lemon juice

2 tablespoons dry white wine

1 teaspoon olive oil

1 tablespoon chopped fresh thyme

1 teaspoon grated fresh ginger

1 teaspoon sugar

Place fish in large shallow dish; pour over combined remaining ingredients. Cover; refrigerate 3 hours or overnight.

Remove fish from marinade; discard marinade. Wrap fish individually in large pieces of foil. Seal foil to enclose fish; transfer to large baking dish. Bake in moderate oven about 25 minutes or until fish is cooked through.

Per serving fat 1.9g; kJ 591

baked fish

with sweet and sour sauce

800g whole snapper

2 tablespoons fish
sauce

cooking oil spray

**sweet and sour
sauce**

2 tablespoons water

2 cloves garlic,
crushed

1/4 teaspoon ground
ginger

pinch chilli powder

1/4 cup (60ml) water,
extra

2 tablespoons brown
sugar

2 tablespoons white
vinegar

2 tablespoons fish
sauce

1 large tomato (250g),
chopped

1 small yellow
capsicum (150g),
chopped

4 baby carrots (80g),
chopped

Make 4 deep diagonal cuts both sides of fish;
pour fish sauce into cuts.

Coat large flameproof baking dish with cooking
oil spray; cook fish, until browned both sides.

Bake fish, covered, in moderate oven about
30 minutes or until cooked through. Serve with
Sweet and Sour Sauce.

Sweet and Sour Sauce Cook water, garlic,
ginger and chilli in large non-stick pan, stirring,
until fragrant. Stir in extra water and remaining
ingredients; simmer, covered, about 3 minutes
or until vegetables are just tender.

Per serving fat 2.7g; kJ 738

30 fish cottage
pie

Boil, steam or microwave potato and pumpkin until tender, drain. Add milk; mash until smooth.

Melt butter in large non-stick pan; cook onion, stirring, until soft. Add the vegetables, extra milk, crumbled stock cube and blended flour and water; stir over heat, until mixture boils and thickens. Add fish; pour mixture into 1.25-litre (5-cup) ovenproof dish; top with potato mixture; sprinkle with cheese.

Bake, uncovered, in moderate oven about 30 minutes or until fish is cooked through and top is browned.

2 medium potatoes (400g), peeled, chopped

200g piece pumpkin, peeled, chopped

2 tablespoons skim milk

15g butter

1 medium brown onion (150g), chopped

2 cups (270g) frozen mixed vegetables, thawed

1/2 cup (125ml) skim milk, extra

1 large vegetable stock cube

2 tablespoons plain flour

1/4 cup (60ml) water

600g white fish fillets, chopped roughly

2 tablespoons finely grated parmesan cheese

Per serving fat 9.2g; kJ 1461

steamed whole fish with
ginger sauce

1 medium carrot (120g)

1 celery stick (75g)

1 small red capsicum (150g)

1 small green capsicum (150g)

4 x 250g whole white fish

ginger sauce

1 tablespoon grated fresh ginger

2 tablespoons mirin

1 tablespoon light soy sauce

2 tablespoons dry sherry

2 teaspoons cornflour

1 cup (250ml) water

3 green onions, chopped

Cut carrot, celery and capsicums into thin strips. Boil, steam or microwave vegetables until just tender; drain.

Fill cavity of each fish with vegetables, secure openings with toothpicks. Place fish, in single layer, on rack, in large flameproof baking dish. Add enough water to baking dish to steam fish, without allowing fish to touch water; bring water to boil. Steam, covered, about 10 minutes or until fish is cooked through. Remove toothpicks; serve fish with Ginger Sauce.

Ginger Sauce Combine ginger, mirin, sauce, sherry and blended cornflour and water in small pan. Stir over heat until sauce boils and thickens slightly. Stir in onion.

Per serving fat 4g; kJ 802

32 the new chip

You can't have fish without chips, but deep-fried chips are scandalously high in fat. Here are four delicious low-fat alternatives.

kipfler potato cakes

1kg kipfler potatoes, peeled

1 clove garlic, crushed

1 teaspoon lemon pepper seasoning

½ cup (960g) finely grated low-fat cheddar cheese

2 tablespoons low-fat sour cream

Boil, steam or microwave potato until just tender; drain.
Mash potato; combine with remaining ingredients in large bowl, cool. Using hands, shape ⅓ cup of mixture into a thick patty; repeat with remaining mixture.
Cook patties, in batches, in heated oiled large pan until lightly browned both sides and heated through.

Per serving fat 5.9g; kJ 986

potato wedges

6 large potatoes (1.8kg)

2 egg whites, beaten lightly

2 tablespoons garlic salt

Boil, steam or microwave unpeeled potatoes until just tender; drain. Cut potatoes into wedges; combine in large bowl with egg white and garlic salt.

Place wedges, in single layer, on oiled oven trays.
Bake, uncovered in very hot oven about 30 minutes or until browned and crisp.

Per serving fat 0.4g; kJ 1076

pink-eye potato crisps

4 medium pink-eye potatoes (425g)

cooking oil spray

Slice unpeeled potato thinly, rinse well, pat dry with absorbent paper. Line oven trays with baking paper, place slices, in single layer, on trays; spray with oil.

Bake in hot oven about 20 minutes or until crisps are browned and crunchy.

Per serving fat 0.8g; kJ 290

oven-baked chips

1 kg potatoes

cooking oil spray

sea salt

Wash the peeled potatoes, cut them into chips (thin or fat, as desired). Dry them very well with paper towels or a clean tea towel. Coat a shallow oven tray with cooking oil spray. Spread chips on the tray in a single layer and coat them well with cooking oil spray; sprinkle with salt.

Cook, uncovered, in very hot oven for 20 to 30 minutes, or until chips are cooked through and brown. Serve immediately.

Per serving fat 1g; kJ 689

From left: kipfler potato cakes; potato wedges; pink-eye potato crisps; oven-baked chips.

34 gremolata fish on
pumpkin rice

1/2 cup chopped fresh flat-leaf parsley

1 tablespoon finely grated lemon rind

3 cloves garlic, crushed

4 white fish fillets (800g)

cooking oil spray

1 bunch silverbeet (1kg), trimmed

2 tablespoons lemon juice

pumpkin rice

1kg butternut pumpkin, peeled, chopped

2 teaspoons ground cumin

1 teaspoon vegetable oil

1 cup (200g) white long-grain rice

2 cloves garlic, crushed

2 cups (500ml) water

Combine parsley, rind and garlic in bowl; press onto fish. Coat large non-stick pan with cooking oil spray; cook fish, until browned both sides and just cooked through.

Boil, steam or microwave silverbeet until just wilted; drain.

Serve Pumpkin Rice topped with silverbeet and fish. Drizzle with juice.

Pumpkin Rice Combine pumpkin, cumin and oil in non-stick baking dish. Bake, uncovered, in very hot oven, about 30 minutes or until pumpkin is tender and just browned. Combine rice, garlic and the water in medium heavy-based pan; bring to boil. Simmer, covered, over low heat, about 10 minutes or until rice is tender and water absorbed. Stir in pumpkin.

Per serving fat 9.5g; kJ 2161

baked fish in chilli
balsamic marinade

2 x 1kg whole snapper

3 cloves garlic, crushed

1 tablespoon chopped fresh rosemary

2 green onions, chopped

2 small fresh red chillies, chopped finely

1 tablespoon sugar

¼ cup (60ml) balsamic vinegar

1 cup (250ml) water

Cut 4 deep diagonal cuts both sides of each fish. Combine remaining ingredients and pour over fish in large shallow dish. Cover; refrigerate 3 hours or overnight.

Place fish in large flameproof baking dish; pour over marinade. Bake, uncovered, in moderately hot oven about 30 minutes or until just cooked through. Remove fish from dish, cover to keep warm.

Simmer juices in pan, uncovered, about 2 minutes or until thickened slightly; pour over fish.

Per serving fat 3.1g; kJ 867

44 baked
chilli snapper

1.5kg whole snapper

2 medium red onions (340g), chopped finely

2 small fresh red chillies, chopped finely

6 cloves garlic, crushed

1 cup (250ml) white vinegar

2 cups (500ml) water

2 tablespoons sugar

2 tablespoons chopped fresh coriander leaves

3 green onions, chopped

Make 3 shallow diagonal cuts both sides of fish, place in large baking dish. Pour combined remaining ingredients over fish. Bake, uncovered, in hot oven about 30 minutes or until fish is cooked. **Remove** fish from dish, cover to keep warm. Strain onion mixture over medium bowl; reserve 1 cup (250ml) cooking liquid. Blend or process onion mixture with reserved cooking liquid, reheat, serve sauce with fish.

Per serving fat 3.4g; kJ 1111

with prosciutto

12 slices prosciutto
(180g)

4 x 230g whole red
mullet

cooking oil spray

2 cloves garlic,
crushed

4 small ripe tomatoes
(520g), sliced thickly

1/4 cup shredded fresh
basil leaves

1 tablespoon drained
capers

Wrap 3 slices of prosciutto firmly around each fish. Coat large non-stick
pan with cooking oil spray, heat pan; cook fish, in batches, about
2 minutes each side or until prosciutto is browned. Place fish in shallow
ovenproof dish.

Cook garlic in same pan, stirring, until fragrant. Add tomato; cook,
uncovered, about 5 minutes, stirring occasionally, or until mixture is thick
and pulpy. Stir in basil and capers.

Spoon tomato mixture over fish; bake, covered, in moderate oven about
20 minutes or until fish is cooked through.

Per serving fat 9.9g; kJ 933

glossary

belacan dried shrimp paste sold in slabs or flat cakes.

breadcrumbs

packaged: fine-textured, crunchy, purchased, white breadcrumbs.

stale: 1- or 2-day-old bread, white or wholemeal made into crumbs by grating, blending or processing.

buttermilk low-fat milk cultured to give a slightly sour, tangy taste; low-fat yogurt can be substituted.

cajun seasoning used to give an authentic spicy Cajun flavour to food, this packaged blend of assorted herbs and spices can include paprika, basil, onion, fennel, thyme, cayenne and tarragon.

capsicum also known as bell pepper or, simply, pepper. Seeds and membranes should be discarded.

choy sum also known as flowering bok choy or flowering white cabbage.

couscous a fine, grain-like cereal product, originally from North Africa; made from semolina.

fish

blue-eye: also known as deep sea trevalla or trevally and blue eye cod; thick, moist white-fleshed fish.

leatherjacket: also known as file fish; has white soft flesh with a mild flavour.

ocean trout: a farmed fish with pink, soft flesh, it is from the same family as the Atlantic salmon.

redfish: small fish, usually sold as skinless fillets; has a pale pink flesh with a delicate flavour.

red mullet: a member of the goatfish family; small firm-fleshed rich-tasting fish.

salmon: red-pink firm flesh; moist delicate flavour.

sea bream: available whole or in fillets; has sweet white fine-textured flesh.

smoked fish: some varieties are smoked trout, mackerel, haddock, kipper and New Zealand blue cod, available from delicatessens and supermarkets.

snapper: small, firm-fleshed, distinct-tasting fish sold whole, good for any kind of cooking method; a number of varieties include red, pink and yellowtail snapper.

tuna: reddish, firm flesh; slightly dry, no bones.

white fish: means non-oily fish. This category includes bream, flathead, whiting, snapper, jewfish, ling and redfish.

fish sauce also called nam pla or nuoc nam; made from pulverised salted fermented fish, most often anchovies. Has a pungent smell and strong taste; use sparingly in Asian recipes.

frozen mixed vegetables a variety of packaged vegetables that are partially cooked, then frozen.

green ginger wine alcoholic sweet wine infused with finely ground ginger.

lemon grass the white lower part of each stem is chopped and used in Asian cooking or for tea.

mayonnaise, low-fat we used a mayonnaise that was 97% fat free.

mirin a sweet low-alcohol rice wine used in Japanese cooking; sometimes referred to simply as rice wine but should not be confused with sake, the Japanese rice wine made for drinking.

mushrooms

button: small, cultivated white mushrooms having a delicate, subtle flavour.

oyster (abalone): grey-white fan-shaped mushroom.

oil

cooking oil spray: vegetable oil in an aerosol can, available in supermarkets.

olive: a mono-unsaturated oil, especially good for everyday cooking and in salad dressing. "Light" describes the mild flavour, not the fat levels.

peanut: pressed from ground peanuts; most commonly used oil in Asian cooking because of its high smoke point.

sesame: made from roasted, crushed, white sesame seeds; a flavouring rather than a cooking medium.

vegetable: any of a number of oils sourced from plants rather than animal fats.

onion

green: also known as scallion or (incorrectly) shallot; an immature onion picked before the bulb has formed, having a long, bright-green edible stalk.

red: or Spanish onion, a sweet-flavoured, large, purple-red onion that is good eaten raw in salads.

sambal oelek (also ulek or olek) Indonesian in origin; a salty paste made from ground chillies.

snow peas also called mange tout ("eat all").

lemon pepper a blend of crushed black pepper, lemon, herbs and spices.

pimientos canned or bottled peppers.

pine nuts also known as pignoli; small, cream-coloured kernels obtained from the cones of different varieties of pine trees.

prosciutto salted-cured, air-dried (unsmoked), pressed ham; usually sold in paper-thin slices, ready to eat.

pumpkin, butternut pear-shaped with golden skin and orange flesh. Various types can be substituted for one another.

rocket also called arugula, rugula and rucola; a green salad leaf.

squash also known as pattipan, scallopine or summer squash; small, flattish yellow or green thin-skinned squash.

stock 1 cup (250ml) stock is the equivalent of 1 cup (250ml) water plus 1 crumbled stock cube (or 1 teaspoon stock powder).

tabasco sauce brand name of an extremely fiery sauce made from vinegar, hot red peppers and salt.

tamarind sauce if not available, soak about 30g dried tamarind in a cup of hot water for 10 minutes, squeeze pulp and use the flavoured water.

teriyaki marinade a blend of soy sauce, wine, vinegar and spices.

teriyaki sauce a homemade or commercially bottled sauce usually made from soy sauce, mirin, sugar, ginger and other spices; it imparts a distinctive glaze when brushed on fish or meat to be grilled.

tomato

paste: triple-concentrated tomato puree used to flavour soups, stews, sauces and casseroles.

puree: canned pureed tomatoes (not tomato paste). Substitute with fresh peeled and pureed tomatoes.

vinegar

balsamic: authentic only from the province of Modena, Italy; made from a regional wine of white Trebbiano grapes specially processed then aged in antique wooden casks to give the exquisite pungent flavour. Drizzle over grilled or barbecued fish.

rice: made from fermented rice, colourless and flavoured with sugar and salt. Also known as seasoned rice vinegar.

white: made from spirit of cane sugar.

wasabi an Asian horseradish used to make a fiery sauce traditionally served with Japanese raw fish dishes.

yogurt, low-fat, plain we used yogurt with a fat content of less than 0.2%.

zucchini: also known as courgette.

62

index

facts and figures 63

These conversions are approximate only, but the difference between an exact and the approximate conversion of various liquid and dry measures is minimal and will not affect your cooking results.

Measuring equipment
The difference between one country's measuring cups and another's is, at most, within a 2 or 3 teaspoon variance. (For the record, 1 Australian metric measuring cup holds approximately 250ml.) The most accurate way of measuring dry ingredients is to weigh them. For liquids, use a clear glass or plastic jug having metric markings.

Note: NZ, Canada, USA and UK all use 15ml tablespoons. Australian tablespoons measure 20ml.
All cup and spoon measurements are level.

How to measure
When using graduated measuring cups, shake dry ingredients loosely into the appropriate cup. Do not tap the cup on a bench or tightly pack the ingredients unless directed to do so. Level the top of measuring cups and measuring spoons with a knife. When measuring liquids, place a clear glass or plastic jug having metric markings on a flat surface to check accuracy at eye level.

Dry Measures

metric	imperial
15g	1/2oz
30g	1oz
60g	2oz
90g	3oz
125g	4oz (1/4lb)
155g	5oz
185g	6oz
220g	7oz
250g	8oz (1/2lb)
280g	9oz
315g	10oz
345g	11oz
375g	12oz (3/4lb)
410g	13oz
440g	14oz
470g	15oz
500g	16oz (1lb)
750g	24oz (1 1/2lb)
1kg	32oz (2lb)

We use large eggs having an average weight of 60g.

Liquid Measures

metric	imperial
30ml	1 fluid oz
60ml	2 fluid oz
100ml	3 fluid oz
125ml	4 fluid oz
150ml	5 fluid oz (1/4 pint/1 gill)
190ml	6 fluid oz
250ml (1cup)	8 fluid oz
300ml	10 fluid oz (1/2 pint)
500ml	16 fluid oz
600ml	20 fluid oz (1 pint)
1000ml (1litre)	1 3/4 pints

Helpful Measures

metric	imperial
3mm	1/8in
6mm	1/4in
1cm	1/2in
2cm	3/4in
2.5cm	1in
6cm	2 1/2in
8cm	3in
20cm	8in
23cm	9in
25cm	10in
30cm	12in (1ft)

Oven Temperatures

These oven temperatures are only a guide. Always check the manufacturer's manual.

	C°(Celsius)	F°(Fahrenheit)	Gas Mark
Very slow	120	250	1
Slow	150	300	2
Moderately slow	160	325	3
Moderate	180 –190	350 – 375	4
Moderately hot	200 – 210	400 – 425	5
Hot	220 – 230	450 – 475	6
Very hot	240 – 250	500 – 525	7

Food editor Pamela Clark
Associate food editor Karen Hammial
Assistant food editor Kathy McGarry
Assistant recipe editor Elizabeth Hooper

HOME LIBRARY STAFF
Editor-in-chief Mary Coleman
Marketing manager Nicole Pizanis
Editor Susan Tomnay
Concept design Jackie Richards
Designer Jackie Richards
Group publisher Tim Trumper
Chief executive officer John Alexander

Produced by *The Australian Women's Weekly*
Home Library, Sydney.

Colour separations by
ACP Colour Graphics Pty Ltd, Sydney.
Printing by Diamond Press Limited, Sydney.

Published by ACP Publishing Pty Limited,
54 Park St, Sydney; GPO Box 4088, Sydney,
NSW 1028. Ph: (02) 9282 8618
Fax: (02) 9267 9438.

AWWHomeLib@publishing.acp.com.au

Australia Distributed by Network Distribution
Company, GPO Box 4088, Sydney, NSW 1028.
Ph: (02) 9282 8777 Fax: (02) 9264 3278.

United Kingdom Distributed by Australian
Consolidated Press (UK), Moulton Park
Business Centre, Red House Rd, Moulton Park,
Northampton, NN3 6AQ. Ph: (01604) 497 531
Fax: (01604) 497 533 Acpukltd@aol.com

Canada Distributed by Whitecap Books Ltd,
351 Lynn Ave, North Vancouver, BC, V7J 2C4,
Ph: (604) 980 9852.

New Zealand Distributed by Netlink Distribution
Company, 17B Hargreaves St, Level 5,
College Hill, Auckland 1, Ph: (9) 302 7616.

South Africa Distributed by PSD Promotions
(Pty) Ltd,PO Box 1175, Isando 1600, SA,
Ph: (011) 392 6065.
CNA Limited, Newsstand Division, PO Box
10799, Johannesburg 2000. Ph: (011) 491 7500.

Healthy Eating: Fish

Includes index.
ISBN 1 86396 148 8.

1. Cookery (Fish). I Title: Australian Women's
Weekly.
(Series: Australian Women's Weekly healthy
eating mini series).
641.692

© ACP Publishing Pty Limited 1999
ACN 053 273 546

Cover: Baked Whiting, page 23 (fish supplied by
The Bondi Surf Seafoods, Bondi Beach, NSW)
Stylist Jane Collins
Photographer Scott Cameron
Back cover: Gremolata Fish, page 34